I0190924

ANIMALS
That Make a Difference!

Primates

Ashley Lee

Explore other books at:
WWW.ENGAGEBOOKS.COM

VANCOUVER, B.C.

e→ WWW.ENGAGEBOOKS.COM

Primates: Level 2
Animals That Make a Difference!
Lee, Ashley 1995 –
Text © 2020 Engage Books
Design © 2020 Engage Books

Edited by: A.R. Roumanis and Lauren Dick
Design by: A.R. Roumanis

Text set in Arial Regular.
Chapter headings set in Arial Black.

FIRST EDITION / FIRST PRINTING

All rights reserved. No part of this book
may be stored in a retrieval system, reproduced
or transmitted in any form or by any other means
without written permission from the publisher
or a licence from the Canadian Copyright Licensing
Agency. Critics and reviewers may quote brief passages in
connection with a review or critical article in any media.

Every reasonable effort has been made to contact the
copyright holders of all material reproduced in this book.

LIBRARY AND ARCHIVES CANADA CATALOGUING IN PUBLICATION

Title: Primates: Animals That Make a Difference Level 2 reader / Ashley Lee
Names: Lee, Ashley, 1995- author

Identifiers: Canadiana (print) 2020030898x | Canadiana (ebook) 20200308998
ISBN 978-1-77437-641-6 (hardcover)
ISBN 978-1-77437-642-3 (softcover)
ISBN 978-1-77437-643-0 (pdf)
ISBN 978-1-77437-644-7 (epub)
ISBN 978-1-77437-645-4 (kindle)

Subjects:
LCSH: Primates—Juvenile literature
LCSH: Human-animal relationships—Juvenile literature

Classification: LCC QL737.P9 L44 2020 | DDC J599.8—DC23

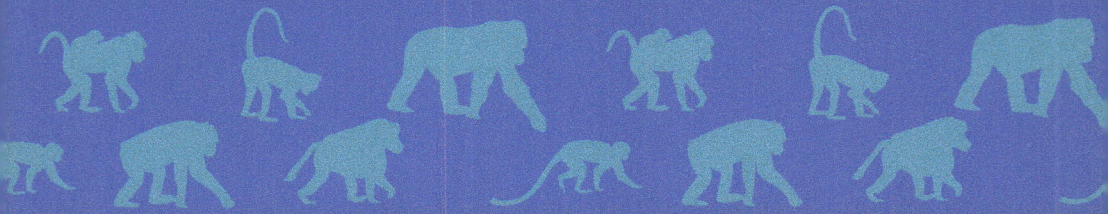

Contents

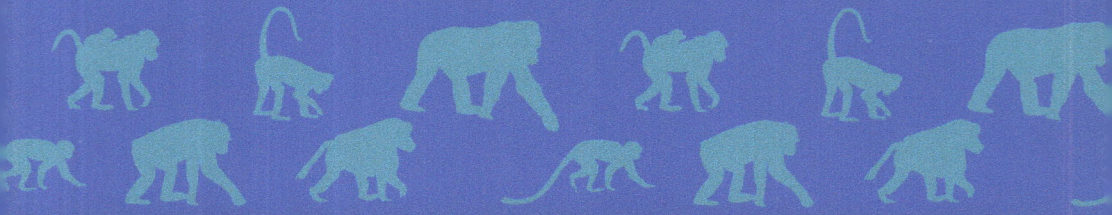

What Are Primates?

Primates are **mammals**.
They have large brains.

KEY WORD

Mammals: animals with warm blood and bones in their backs.

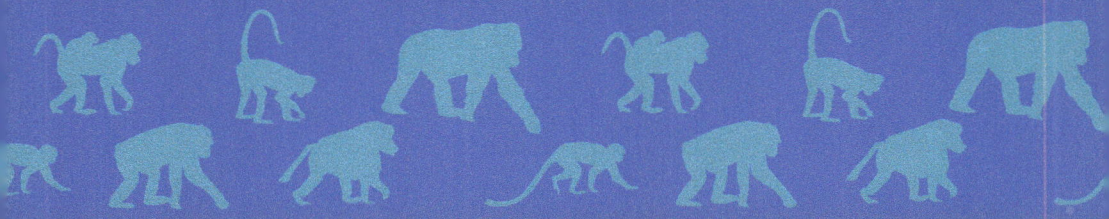

Most primates can grip things with their feet. They are very helpful to people, other animals, and Earth.

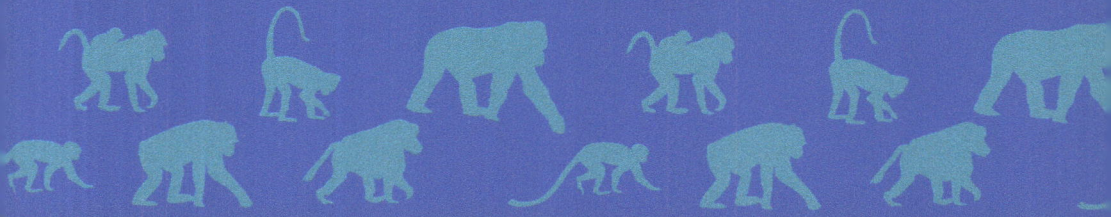

A Closer Look

The smallest primates are mouse lemurs. They are only about 3.5 inches (9 centimeters) long. Gorillas are the largest primates. They can be up to 5.5 feet (1.7 meters) long.

Most primates have sharp teeth called canines. They are used for eating and scaring other animals away.

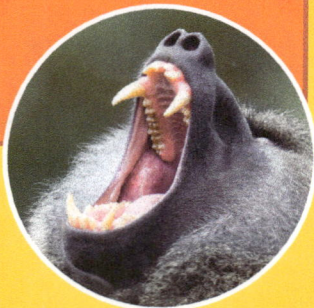

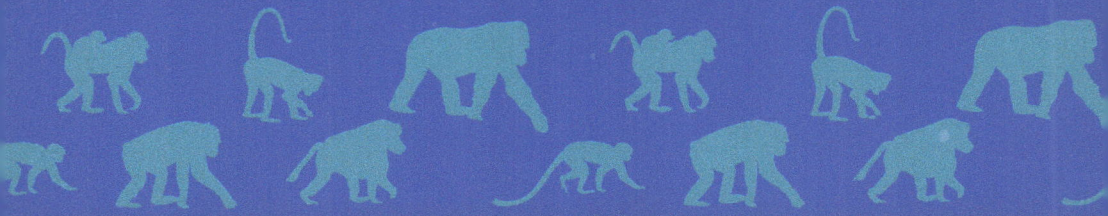

Some primates have tails that can hold onto things. These tails act like an extra arm.

Most primates have thumbs on all four feet. Thumbs help primates hold things.

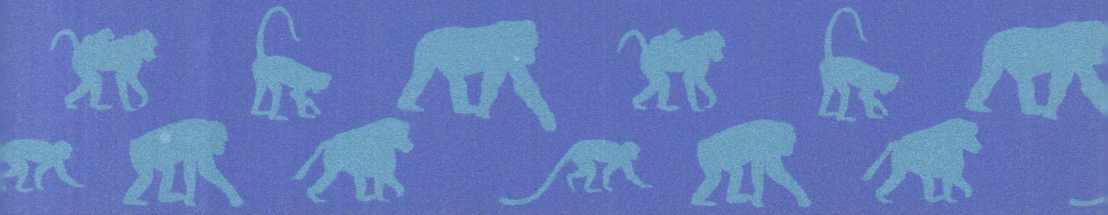

Where Do Primates Live?

Primates live in forest or grassland **habitats**. Most primates are social animals. They live together in groups.

KEY WORD

Habitats: the places a plant or animal lives. Different animals need different habitats.

Primates live in Africa, Asia, and South America. Lemurs are only found in Madagascar. Orangutans live in Indonesia. Lion tamarins live in rainforests in Brazil.

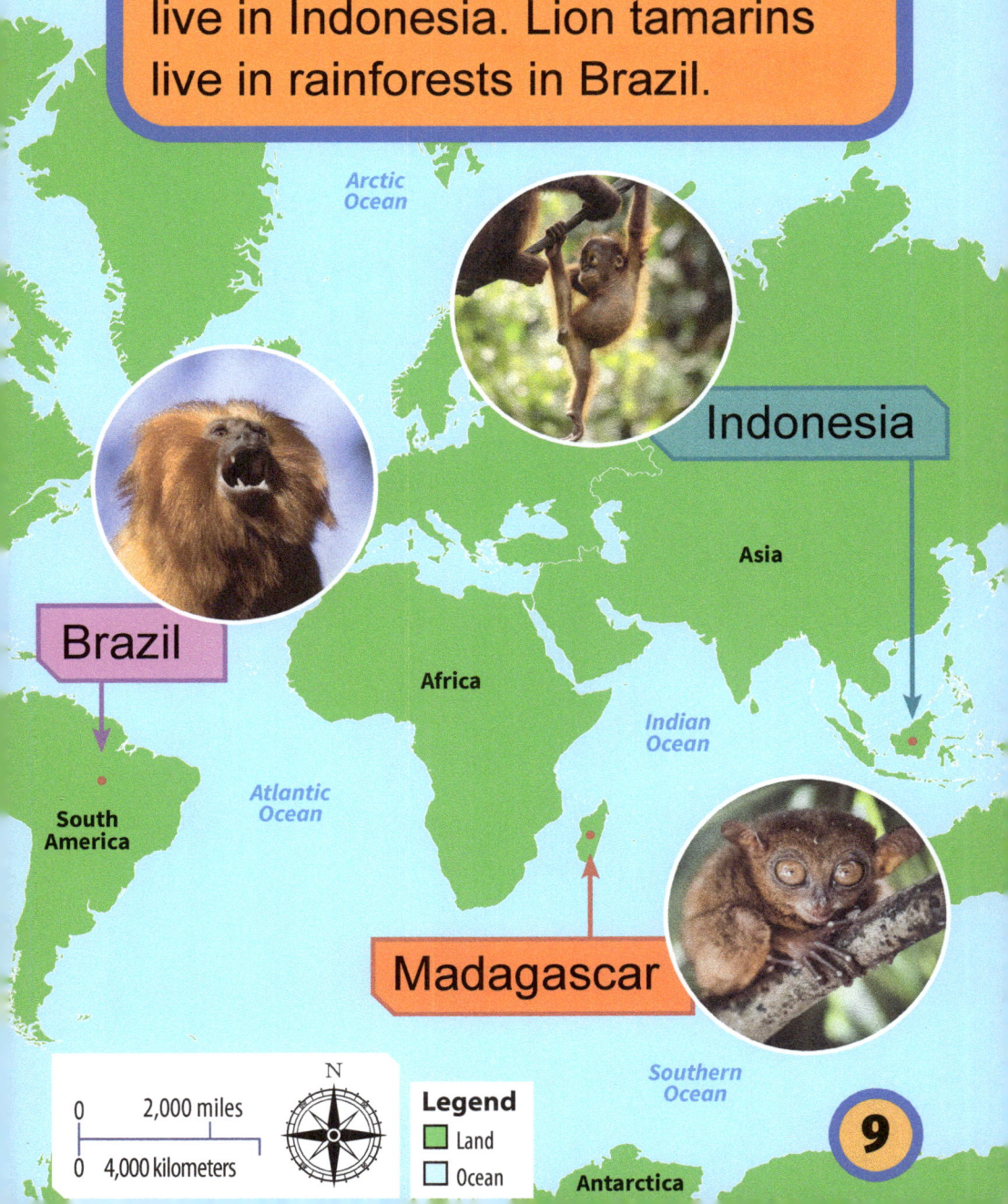

Arctic Ocean

Indonesia

Asia

Brazil

Africa

Indian Ocean

Atlantic Ocean

South America

Madagascar

Southern Ocean

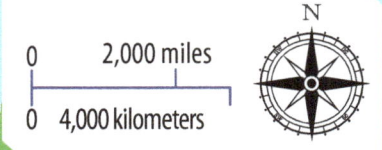

Legend
Land
Ocean

0   2,000 miles
0   4,000 kilometers

N

Antarctica

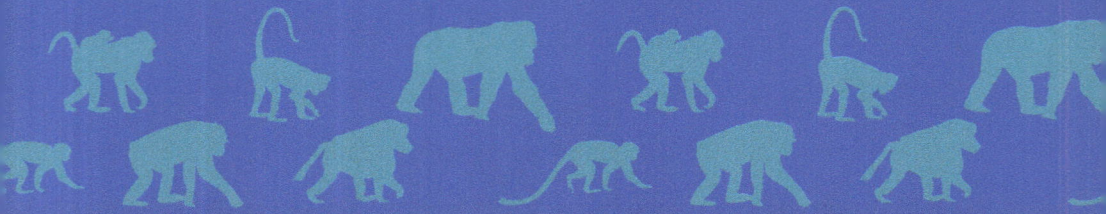

What Do Primates Eat?

Primates eat both plants and meat. Some primates eat more plants than meat. They eat fruit, leaves, nuts, and grass.

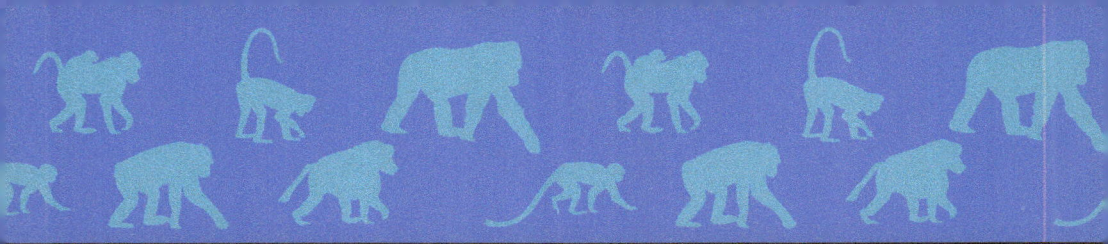

Other primates eat a lot of meat. Insects, birds, and frogs are all important primate foods.

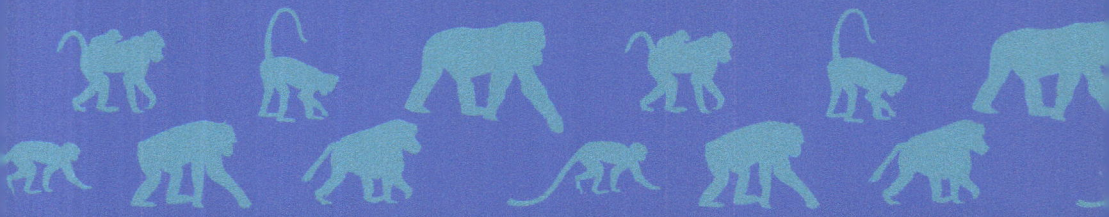

How Do Primates Talk to Each Other?

Primates use calls and body movements to let others know how they feel. A growl may show anger. Pointing to the sky can warn others of a dangerous bird nearby.

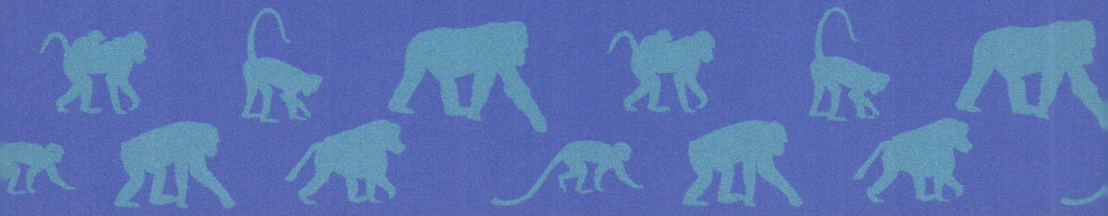

Some primates have been taught **sign language** by humans. One gorilla learned more than 1,000 sign language words.

KEY WORD

Sign language: making words with hand and body movements.

Primate Life Cycle

Most primates are born with their eyes open. They are already covered in hair. Many mothers carry their babies with them when they look for food.

Primates stay with their mothers for 2 to 10 years. Mothers groom their children and teach them how to find food.

Some primates live longer than others. Lemurs live for about 15 years. Chimpanzees can live for up to 60 years.

Curious Facts About Primates

Primates clean each other's fur. They eat any bugs they find hiding in the fur.

Primates use tools. They will use a rock to open nuts or leaves to clean their ears.

Chimpanzees use special plants to treat their injuries.

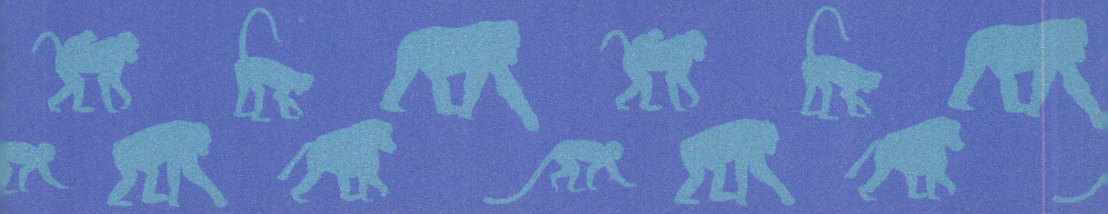

Howler monkeys are one of the loudest monkeys. They can be heard from 3 miles (5 km) away.

Some monkeys clean their fruits and vegetables before eating them.

Humans are primates.

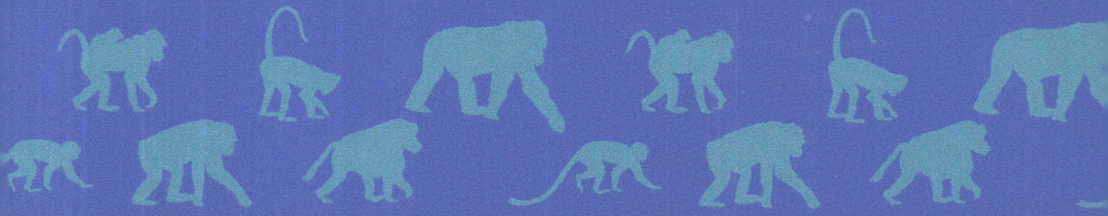

Kinds of Primates

There are more than 300 kinds of primates. New kinds of primates continue to be found. Scientists have found more than 35 new kinds of primates since the year 2000.

Cotton-top tamarins are about the size of a squirrel. They mostly give birth to twins.

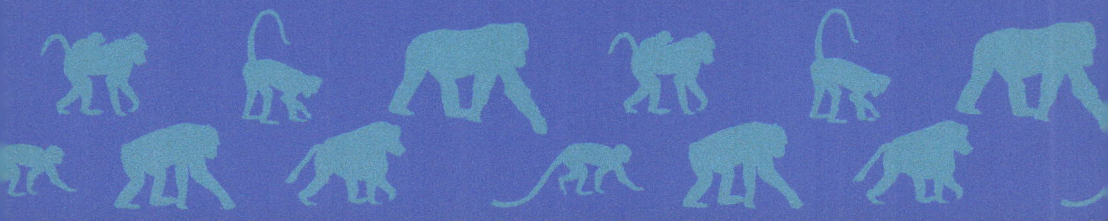

Mandrills are brightly colored. They have pouches in their cheeks that store food for later.

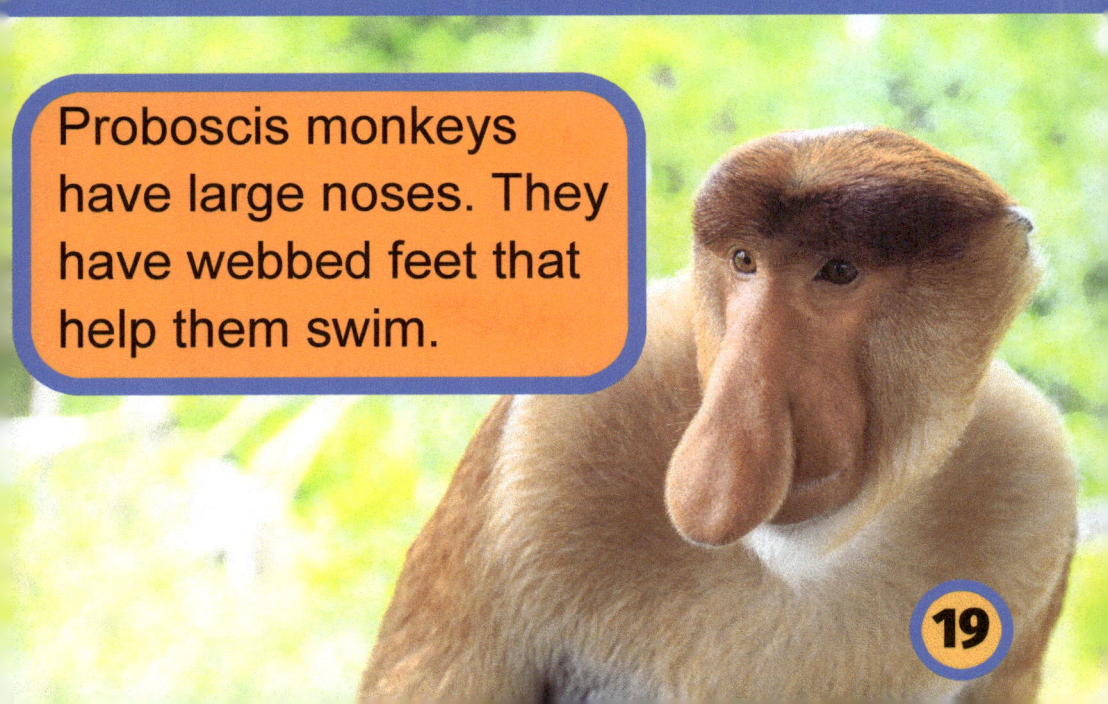

Proboscis monkeys have large noses. They have webbed feet that help them swim.

How Primates Help Earth

Primates eat lots of fruit that are filled with seeds. The seeds come out in their poop. Primates spread seeds to new areas when they travel.

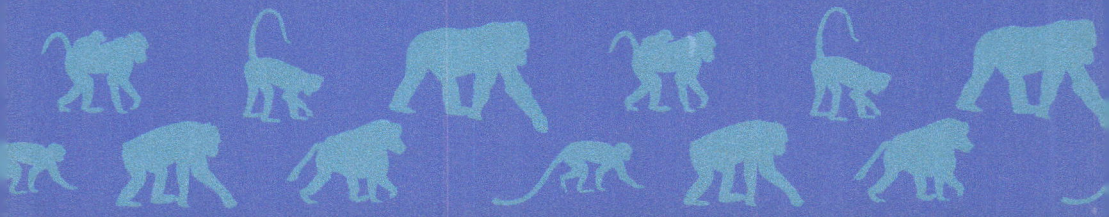

Primate poop fertilizes the seeds to help them grow into new plants. Many forests need primates to help them grow bigger.

How Primates Help Other Animals

Many animals eat the leaves and fruits from plants that primates help grow. There would not be as much food for other animals to eat without primates.

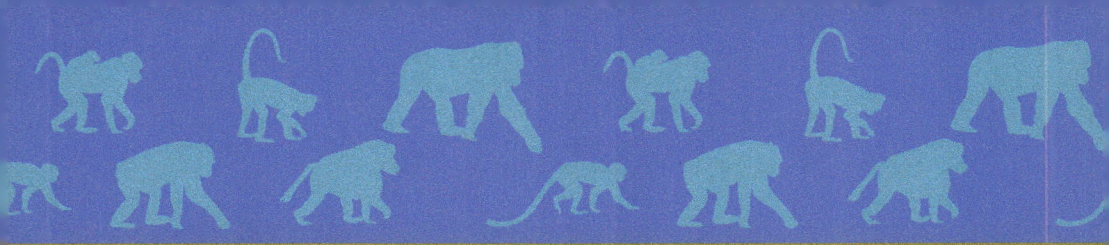

Smaller primates are an important source of food for other animals. Leopards, snakes, and lizards all eat primates. Less primates would mean less food for these animals.

How Primates Help Humans

Humans share **ancestors** with other primates. Studying other primates helps scientists know where humans came from.

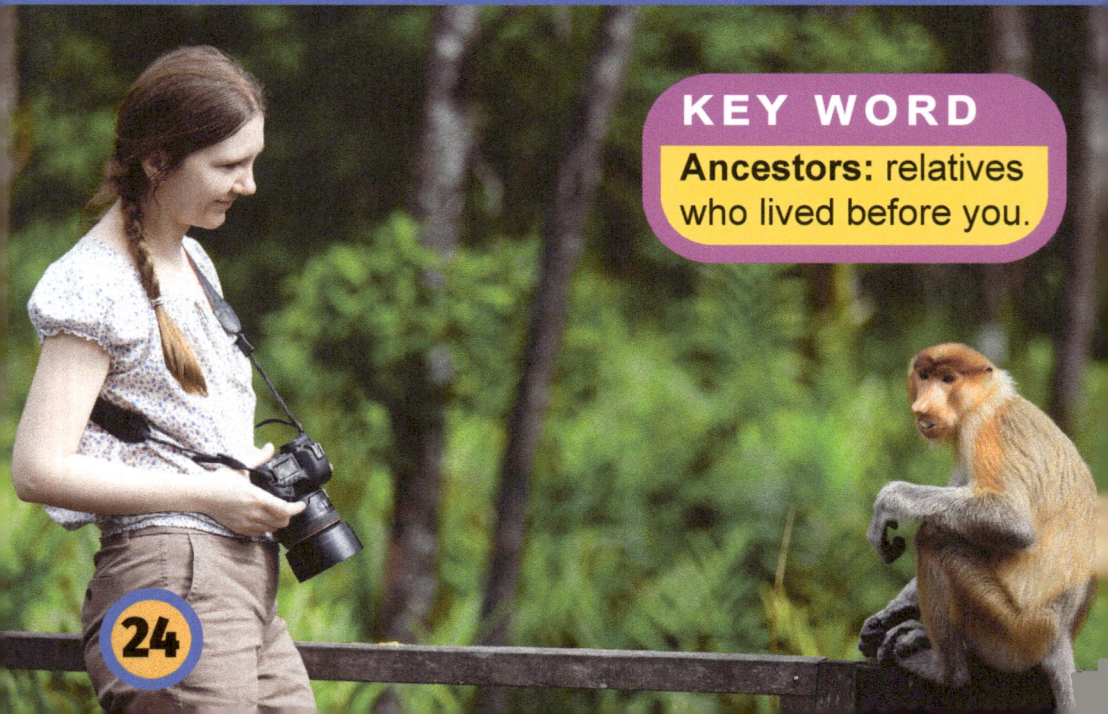

KEY WORD

Ancestors: relatives who lived before you.

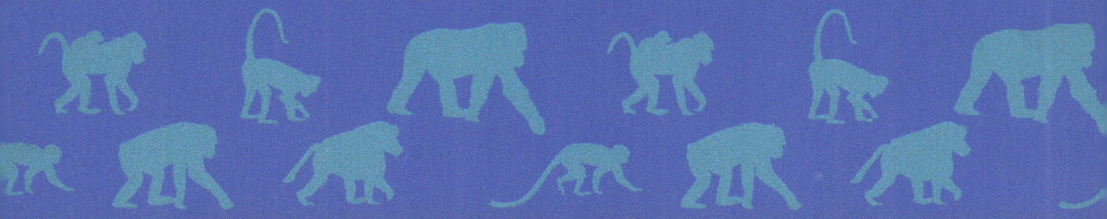

Many primates have similar brains to humans. Scientists study wild primates to learn about human behaviour. They are able to study how humans first started using tools. They can also learn about how mental illnesses develop.

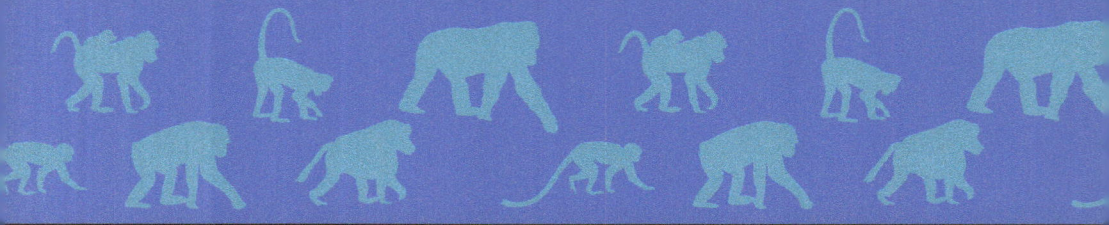

Primates in Danger

Many primates are endangered. This means there are very few of them left.

Orangutans and gorillas are losing their habitats. Growing cities and logging force these animals out of their homes.

Some primates have gone extinct. This means there are no more left.

Miss Waldron's red colobus monkey went extinct in 2000. It was the first primate to go extinct in more than 200 years.

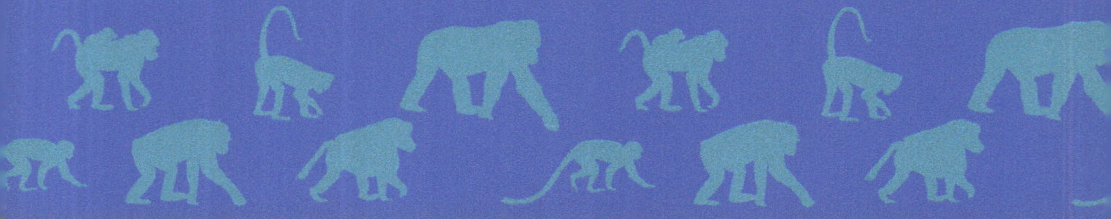

How To Help Primates

Primates can get stuck in pieces of garbage they find. This can hurt them as they try to get free. Some primates will try to eat garbage. This can make them very sick.

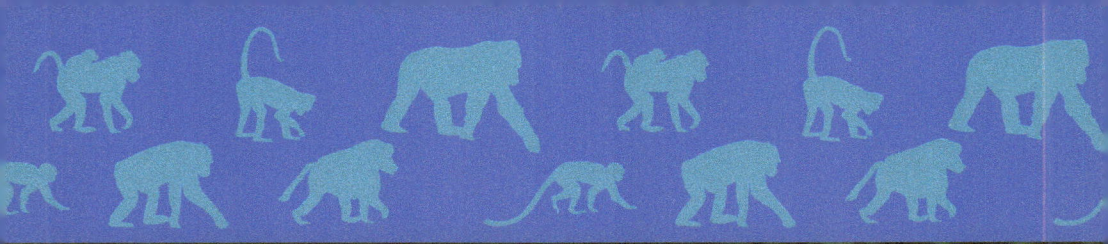

Many people are organizing forest clean-ups. Removing garbage from primate habitats can help save them.

Quiz

Test your knowledge of primates by answering the following questions. The questions are based on what you have read in this book. The answers are listed on the bottom of the next page.

1 Where do primates live?

2 What do primates eat?

3 How do primates talk to each other?

4 How long do lemurs live?

5 What animals eat primates?

6 What is forcing orangutans and gorillas out of their homes?

Explore other books in the Animals That Make a Difference series.

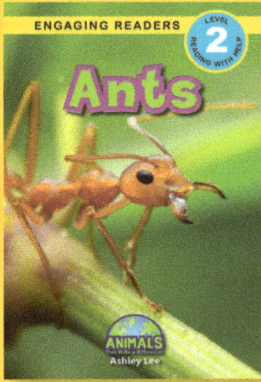

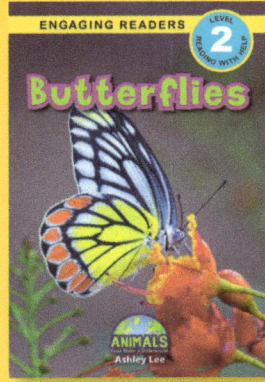

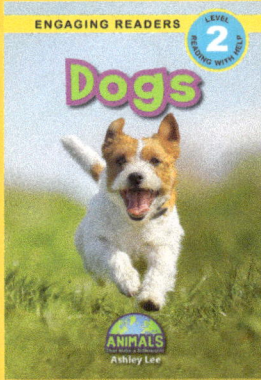

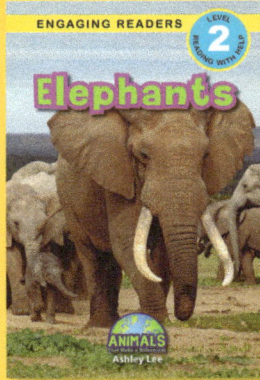

Visit www.engagebooks.com to explore more Engaging Readers.

Answers: 1. Forests or grasslands 2. Plants and meat 3. They use calls and body language 4. About 15 years 5. Leopards, snakes, and lizards 6. Growing cities, forest fires, and logging